I0059700

WE ARE
ALL
MILLIONAIRES

Second Edition

By Semisi Pone

BSc, MSc (Hons)

Copyright © Rainbow Enterprises 2014

Publisher: Rainbow Enterprises 2014

ISBN: 978-1-927308-27-1

All rights reserved. No part of this publication shall be reproduced in any way without prior written permission from the copyright holder and publisher. Rainbow Enterprises in the trade/publisher name of Semisi Pule a.k.a. Semisi Pule Pone.

2nd Edition

Email: rainbowenterprises7@gmail.com

Distributed by Rainbow Enterprises

CONTENTS

INTRODUCTION.

It is an interesting notion, to think that we all have the potential to be millionaires but we are not. Simply because our leaders or the leaders of the countries of the world have not come up with a brilliant idea to make it happen. It will solve a lot of problems if we are all wealthy.

Start with the poverty related problems of hunger, disease, no shelter and clothes. Add unemployment and economic crises. Unemployment alone is responsible for many of the poverty problems in the West. There are about 50-60 million unemployed people in the United States, European Union, Australia and New Zealand. This number changes with each successive Government's fortunes but it shows the huge effect it will have on the welfare of the State. It will cost billions of dollars for the State to look after its unemployed citizens.

In addition, the free services the Governments provide like health, education and others puts a huge strain on their budgets. For example, some patients in New Zealand hospitals have been quoted in the news media to cost the State more than $2 million for their hospital care. I am sure it is the same in most developed countries.

The State has many other problems with provision of services and it seems there is no quick fix for it.

Some ideas will be suggested in this book.

In addition, there are suggestions for unemployed people who want to look at options other than employment. Like starting a business, for example. This has been proposed in my book **"If you can't find a job start a business"**.

Some ideas for a "life plan" are also suggested. It is a good idea to have a plan of where you want to be in 5, 10, 15, 20 years time. It does not have to be a detailed plan but a rough idea of where you want your career to end when you retire.

CHAPTER 1. HOW MUCH ARE YOU WORTH?

Everyone on earth is born with 104,000 hours of working time, if you start working at 16 and retire at 67 years old. If you sell these hours to an employer at the minimum wage of $NZ14 per hour, that will be $NZ 1,456,000. Your total income of a lifetime. If this is your equity in a property, you are a millionaire already! Even before you start working! The question is, how can you convert this asset into cash to help you when you are not working? Is it possible to trade "Labour assets" or "Working hours" on the Stock Market?

If you are trained, you will be worth more. Perhaps $NZ 20 per hour for a junior clerk. $NZ 70 per hour for an electrician, plumber, mechanic or carpenter. $NZ100 per hour for Bachelor degree holders and $NZ200 for Masters degree holders. $NZ300 per hour for PhD holders. It would be worth all the years of training and the expenses as a student if your degree "worth" can be traded on the Stock market like "shares". The experts should come up with a trading system that can use your skills "worth" to leverage your income when "unemployed". Perhaps you can trade it for cash and use it as capital to start a business.

Billionaires like Bill Gates and Warren Beatty have given $US30 billion to charity, according to the news media. This money is used to help improve "global health" and alleviate poverty as reported by Bill Gates's Facebook page. But does that go far enough? Is the problem really poverty and health? Or the inability of the individuals to look after themselves?

Let's pose a hypothetical question that everyone on earth can convert their "labour assets" of a minimum $NZ1,456,000 into cash at any point in their adult lives. Assuming they are trained to look after that money and invest it for their ongoing maintenance, will he/she have a problem with health and poverty? If every individual on earth has that convertible cash asset, will countries on earth lack funds for development? Probably not.

The problem is that, like the status quo, no one has come up with a brilliant idea to make this happen. Economic theory as it applies to-day does not take this into account.

Many people and nations are too busy fighting each other over things they can't control, they overlook their own welfare.

If the whole world can agree on a system that uses this "labour asset" as well as "brick and mortar" for trading, we can eliminate poverty and all its associated problems for ever.

I cannot see it happening.

The West and the East have been fighting over differences in ideology for more than 1,000 years, it is hard to see how they can agree to trade "labour assets". Unless, the West can take the lead and the world will simply have to follow. If the United States and its allies agree to trade "labour assets" on the stock market, everyone else will have no choice but to follow and adapt it, just like technology and services.

By making its citizens wealthy as a conscious decision of the State, all its problems like unemployment, poverty, poor health and so on will simply disappear.

Education and wealth are the solutions to all of the world's problems, if we can find ways to implement them.

CHAPTER 2. SELLING YOUR TIME

Most people sell their time as their main source of income. $NZ14.00 per hour for the minimum wage. $NZ 560 for 40 hours before tax. You work for your employer for these set amounts of time and you receive the set amount of payment.

For Chief Executive Officers (CEOs), this amount may not be based on an hourly rate. It may be based on an "attractive package" like salary, health insurance, accommodation, kid's education and other factors like moving between countries. Chief Executive salaries range from $NZ 100,000+ for a small company to $NZ5,000,000+ for large corporations.

Larger amounts are stated for countries like the United States where some CEOs earn $US100 million per year plus bonuses.

If you work out the weekly earnings of the guy on the minimum wage and a CEO of a large company, there is a huge difference.

The minimum wage is $NZ560 while the CEO earns $NZ 96,154 per week, if he/she is on $NZ5 million per year. Probably with additional perks. In the USA the CEOs can make $US 1,923,077 per week plus bonuses!

We may ask ourselves the question. Why is there such a huge difference? Surely the person on $NZ560 per week deserve a little more? Obviously he will have to budget every cent while the guy on $2 million a week can fly to Macau or the Bahamas, on a private jet, just to spent the weekend!

We all know CEOs have a larger work load and are responsible for the wealth of the entire company, but surely a better system can be worked out? The person on minimum wage will be suffering from stress because of his money scarcity while the guy on $US2 million a week will be suffering from the trappings of the rich, like obesity, lifestyle diseases and so on. A problem of affluence and too much money.

Maybe selling our time is not the best way to advance our economic welfare.

However, at the moment, there is no alternative.

Like they say about democracy, it is not perfect but it is the best system we have. Some people may argue that in the case of China, communism is the better system.

The Chinese are out performing all the other economies of the world at the moment, so there must be some truth in it. They have had $US700 billion surpluses, or close to it, every year in the last 10 years according to certain news reports; while the other major economies of the world are struggling with billions in deficit. In the case of the USA, trillions of dollars in deficit!.

Uneven distribution of wealth may be the cause of poverty in the West.

CHAPTER 3. THE PROPERTY FORTUNE MYTH.

Buying a house was the most popular investment for most New Zealanders in the past. But it is becoming more and more unattainable for average Kiwis. My uncle's property was worth $40-50,000 when he bought it in 1980. It is now worth more than $1 million, in 2014. His daughter has built another house in the backyard!

If you had bought a house in the 1980s, you would be one of the lucky ones because house prices were generally below $100,000. Now, in the 2000s house prices are way beyond the means of the average wage earner. Average wages, as reported in the media, are around the $50,000 mark but the average house in Auckland is around $500-600,000! Even if you can buy such a house on the average wage, with no deposit, the weekly mortgage would be difficult to meet.

If you are a self employed writer on the

average earning of $14,000 per year, it would be the greatest joke of the century to attempt to purchase a property.

My wife's cousin was living with his family in a State House. They were struggling on one income. He has to mow a few lawns during the weekend to make ends meet.

He was a barman in a city hotel for many years and was involved with the management of the bar in the later years. Lucky for him, Jim Bolger's National Government allowed tenants in State Houses to buy them on a "rent to own" arrangement. He bought his State House, and ten or so years later, he was able to use his equity in the house to buy a bar in the city. A few years later he bought another bar in Otahuhu, a suburb of Auckland. Now he employs the whole family in his business and is making a profit for himself.

But very few New Zealanders are that lucky.

I believe the only way for average and low

income earners in New Zealand to leverage their wealth is for the Government to help.

Kiwisaver was the greatest Government Policy in the past 100 years. It allowed wage earners to save money for their retirement. That is additional to their pension.

I saved more than $10,000 in 3 years on the minimum wage while I was looking for a better paid job. I left and became a writer and has not contributed ever since but it is still earning interest and growing.

My wife who has been contributing since Kiwi Saver started has saved more than $20,000.

If the Governments of the world can introduce such measures to leverage low incomes like "rent to own" houses and properties we may see urban poverty become a distant memory.

My wife's cousin's fortune is proof of that.

The National Government and the Labour Party in New Zealand have promised more houses build to try and reduce the average price to affordable levels. Labour promised 100,000 houses to be build over 10 years for low income earners if it wins the election and become the Government. But it did not go far enough. Low income voters cannot see how they can afford an average house at $500,000, $400,000 or even $300,000!

Voters still prefer the "rent to own" arrangement of the National Government which has now included contributions of $5,000 from Kiwisaver and up to $20,000 Government assistance for a deposit for low income earners.

It showed in the election result, Labour had its worst result in more than 20 years with only 25% of the votes. National got about 50% of the votes.

There were other factors like the popularity of the current Prime Minister, John Key, and the good performance of his Government over the last 6 years, but housing has become a key factor in the voting decisions of many people, including myself.

It is true, New Zealanders view their homes as their fort. It is the closest to their heart after their family, and it will be a major factor in every decision they make including which party will become the Government.

The only way to help low income people is to leverage their wealth by offering affordable "rent to own" arrangements.

CHAPTER 4. THE PROBLEMS OF SMALL BUSINESS

I read a brochure or information leaflet about starting a business in New Zealand in 1996, when I first arrived from Fiji. It stated that 95% of all small businesses in New Zealand fail within the first 2 years. There were reasons given like insufficient funds, bad debts, inexperienced owners and so on.

But I still decided to start a business. I had moved to New Zealand after my first contract with the South Pacific Commission (*SPC is now known as the Secretariat for the Pacific Community with its headquarters in Noumea, New Caledonia*) fell through the "cracks on the floor".

I have not said anything about it in the last 18 years since my contract expired in May 1996. Now, I feel that something should be done about it so that it will never happen again at the regional level. It is inexcusable for staff in regional organisations such as the South Pacific Commission to be treated like those of an insolvent company. You either take the redundancy payment and leave or get "chopped".

All the staff positions on core budget, which is the budget contributed by member countries, were advertised in 1995. Strangely we were all asked to apply again. The rumor was that *there might be better staff out there to replace us.*

The other rumor was *SPC is undergoing restructuring because staff salaries are too high and need to be brought down to "Pacific level". Which I understood to be a reduction from my $F6,000 a month down to $F800 a month if they use the Tongan Government salary scale.*

I applied about 6 months before the end of my contract, before going on my annual leave in April 1996.

Prior to leaving, I was selected to be in the panel to choose the new Manager of our programme, the Agriculture Programme.

There were 2 candidates the panel felt were the most suitable. The incumbent and a French expert from New Caledonia. The panel selected the incumbent to continue from 6 to 9 years. We felt that there is no reason to "chop" him off as he was doing alright.

I heard later the French were not happy with that decision since all core staff are supposed to have a maximum of only 6 years. They felt their man should have been the Manager for the Agriculture Programme according to the "rules" at the time.

The problem was, some other staff have been at SPC for 11 years so there was a precedent and management accepted our recommendation.

I left on my annual leave in April, 1996 and did some tests in Auckland because I was not feeling well. I was told I don't have antibodies to hepatitis B so I agreed to have my vaccination done. It was a 3 injection programme with 3 and six months for the last 2.

I asked our office in Suva for sick leave so I can have the second injection before returning but was told the Manager is out of Suva. It was not the Manager's job but the Administration's. To make a long story short...nothing was done. I was entitled to 3 months sick leave in my contract.

A month or so before the end of my contract in May, I called the big boss in New Caledonia and asked him about my contract and he said he does not know anything about it!

I was feeling a bit disillusioned with the whole setup. They have had 6 months to decide and they have not.

I was not surprised as one of my colleagues have been working for 6 months with no contract. According to the Fiji Government work permit conditions, once the contract expires the visa expires. So my colleague has been working illegally in Fiji for 6 months! He was still paid but he does not have a contract! Imagine a staff   member of a 27 member country organisation like the SPC working illegally with the knowledge of the management?.

Such is the mismanagement of the SPC bosses!

I felt that I should have had my job contract renewed, instead of being advertised. Firstly, because I still had 3 years before the 6 year maximum. Secondly, I was able to attract more than $NZ20 million of funding for our Plant Protection Programmes during my 3 years. I don't think any SPC staff before or since has done that. Of course, I was only part of the SPC team doing this work but I was the co-ordinator and I feel justified to say they owe me another 3 year contract for all that success!

I was also able to co-ordinate the establishment of the Pacific Plant Protection Organisation, with help from the FAO legal adviser, under the auspices of the SPC-Plant

Protection Service after 8 years of discussions!.

My job was still advertised!

I have been told that there is a Plant Protection position advertised by the Food and Agriculture Organisation of the United Nations regional office in Apia, Samoa; so I decided to withdraw my application for the Plant Protection Advisor position at SPC and apply to FAO.

I thought maybe they treat their staff a bit more professionally being the United Nations.

It was delayed by one year, but I did not get the job.

Such is the problem with the "small business" mentality of some people who have the misfortune of becoming a leader in a large organisation without the skills to lead it.

I decided to stay in New Zealand and find a job. After a month of ringing around I realised I have to start a business. There was no job for me in Auckland at that time. A job that pays the kind of salary I want.

I had saved about $NZ30-40,000 from the 3 years I spent in Fiji and I also got paid another $NZ50,000 from our SPC "superannuation". I had already worked out that I can make a good profit from importing Pacific Island produce. Turners and Growers was the largest importer of Pacific Island produce into New Zealand, but there were many products like frozen cassava and other root crops that it did not import. The local root crop importers were small and irregular with poor quality.

I decided to have a go at importing and retailing Pacific Island produce. My aim was to help the small growers in Tonga, Fiji and Samoa market their produce in New Zealand. I had worked in Agriculture in the Pacific for 10 years so I know everything there is to know about it.

I bought a small grocery shop in Royal Oak, a suburb of Auckland, for $NZ16,000 and ordered my first container of frozen cassava from Fiji for $F7,000. I had arranged with a friend to supply me; which would be profitable for both of us.

I started some adverts on the local Pacific Island radio 531 PI and also put some ads in the Tongan and Auckland suburban newspapers.

The first container of frozen cassava arrived one month later. The quality was excellent and I began selling larger amounts from the shop each day. Most customers were Pacific Islanders; Tongans, Niueans, Cook Islanders, Fijians and also Asians. They all loved my Fijian cassava! It was the first time anyone in New Zealand imported it. Most frozen cassava in the Auckland market had been supplied from Tonga with mixed results.

My business trade was roaring ahead with up to $NZ4,000 in sales a week. It included my grocery shop sales and deliveries of fresh vegetables and fruits to local restaurants and frozen cassava to private homes.

I sold the first container of cassava in one month and ordered another one.

Then disaster struck.

I rang a Tongan lawyer and asked about local businesses to invest in. I thought that I can start investing profits from the shop every month and build my business equity quickly.

He told me about a new venture in Henderson. It was a Samoan who was manufacturing concentrated coconut cream for the restaurant and Pacific Island market. He wanted investors because the business was struggling with lack of cash.

I went and had a look at his factory setup and product and was convinced it was a winner. Concentrated coconut cream is a product of the future. Once the 300,000

Pacific Islanders in New Zealand get a taste of it, we will be millionaires in no time. His biggest problem was supply of mature coconuts from the islands. He was importing 20 kg sacks of coconuts from Tuvalu and there were too many problems with the supply. Firstly the irregular shipping and the costs but also the spoilage of the nuts during the long voyage from Tuvalu to Auckland. Add the small volume and you have an unsolvable problem.

His product was supplied in 1 and 2 litre plastic bottles similar to milk bottles. The quality was excellent! The small factory was also clean and well maintained, but he did everything himself with the help of family members. It was labour intensive but I thought the excellent quality and "high demand" for the concentrated coconut cream justifies my investment in his business.

I offered to supply him with one container of coconuts every month so we can boost the sales and generate more cash.

He agreed.

I knew him from the University of Auckland and rugby and so I thought there was no need for a written contract. We just shook hands with a "gentleman's agreement".

I rang my father in Tonga, who had recently retired from the civil service, and arranged to pay him 10 cents per coconut plus shipping. It would be a good business for him in his retirement. He said he will discuss it with his relatives and let me know.

They agreed.

They were able to find some farmers who were willing to supply them the coconuts at 5 cents and they sell it to me at 10 cents each.

I flew to Tonga and bought a $TOP6,000, 3 tonne truck for the old man to collect the coconuts with. His pickup was too small for the job.

I arranged to sell the coconuts to the Henderson factory at 30 cents each. The fruit shop prices in Auckland was about $NZ1-1.40 per coconut so 30 cents was a good price for the factory.

The first container arrived from Tonga with 30,000 coconuts in the second month. I had paid $TOP 4,000 for it. I hired some helpers and unloaded the container at the Henderson factory.

The concentrated coconut cream was selling well. I got a fridge and sold some of them in the shop with the frozen cassava.

The second container of coconuts arrived in the third month with another 30,000 coconuts. It cost me another $TOP 4,000.

However, unknown to me my friend at the Henderson factory was struggling to pay some previous debts and a loan from the Pacific Business Trust or a similar establishment.

It was the beginning of the end.

My Samoan friend was unable to find any further funds. He was servicing his loans with the income from my containers of coconuts.

He was unable to pay me my $NZ16,000 invoice. I had spent a total of $NZ12,000 and will only make a small profit from it. I was hoping to help him recover and become profitable because the product was obviously in great demand by the Pacific Island community in Auckland and also the Asian restaurants.

Then another disaster.

Another Tongan business customer ordered a container of frozen cassava from me, which I gave him at a very cheap price. My reasons was the same as the factory. If I can help his business recover, I would have two customers ordering 2 containers from me every month. That would be an easy profit of $NZ10,000-12,000 every month on top of my shop sales.

He also reneged on payment.

I was now out of pocket by $NZ22,000!
Although my shop sales were doing well,
my capital was almost all gone so I was
unable to invest any amounts larger than my
weekly profit.

My Dad and relatives were devastated. They
had big dreams for their coconut business
but everything is now falling apart. I told
them to keep the $TOP6,000 truck.

It was the beginning of the end for my small
business.

I tried everything to recover my cost, even
taking the Samoan factory owner in
Henderson to court and paying the lawyer
$NZ1,700 before he even gets off his desk!
But it was all a waste of time.

There were also 20,000 or so coconuts still
sitting in the factory. All wasted! The owner

of the factory rung me and threatened to sue if I don't remove them as the Samoan tenant had told him they were mine! He wants to put up the factory for rent.

I told him I had sold the containers to the Samoan tenant and invoiced him. Legally he owns the coconuts in the factory and he owes me $NZ16,000 for them!

Somebody also rang me later and offered me some of the factory equipment but I told him they belong to the factory tenant and not me. He has to sell them and pay me the $NZ16,000.

Then I remembered the report I read. My small business has joined the 95% that failed within the first 2 years. It was not my fault. It was bad debt. I should have asked for payment up front.

It was a sad, sad story that is similar to many thousands of other small businesses in New Zealand.

In my case, the problem was that 2 business men, who were struggling with their businesses tried to get their supplies from me for free! It was obvious they made a lot of money from the containers of coconuts and cassava but they spent the money on more urgent debts.

Another added problem was the huge cost of recovering the debt. My lawyer said he can recover all the debt and get them to pay his cost, but I have to pay for his expenses upfront.

I was unable to do that, and despite supplying all the paper work and evidence to the lawyer, he was unable to recover my losses.

I think that is a problem in New Zealand. It is very hard to make debtors pay if they refuse, unless you can pay the lawyers to force them to pay or confiscate their properties and assets to pay you.

So my business, and my friend's, became

statistics, joining the 95% that failed. Such is the problem of small businesses in New Zealand.

Needless to say, the concentrated coconut cream in the New Zealand market is now supplied from Indonesia. It is excellent and very popular with Pacific Islanders. I am sure they will be making millions of dollars from it.

Millions of dollars which should have been earned by our businesses.

Most of the frozen cassava in the New Zealand market now is supplied from Fiji by a large company. They will also make millions of dollars from it.

Millions of dollars which should have been earned by my company.

Sadly, the small operators like myself, my Fijian friend, my Dad, the Henderson factory and the Tongan cassava businessman will lose out to the big operators.

Not because we don't know what to do, but because we failed to help each other to stay in the game. On top of that, it is impossible to get any funding to help your business in that situation, even when you have a product that will sell for millions of dollars.

That is another weakness in the New Zealand business community.

If the New Zealand Government had a facility to help small businesses with potential, many local products will not be lost to overseas competitors.

CHAPTER 5. THE GLOBAL THEORY

In the days of sailing ships the world was a very large place. It took weeks and months to travel from one country to another.

Now, the world has shrunk a thousand times. It takes a few hours to fly from one country to another. You can also talk and see people on the other side of the world in real time. Distance and space does not seem to matter. Only time is the difference.

What goes on in the world is on the news everyday. Every disaster, flood, hurricane, tornado, tsunami, famine, war and plane crashes are displayed on the TV screen in minute detail.

Anyone from anywhere no matter how remote and small their island, are able to reach the rest of the world by phone or on the internet.

For instance, the Tongan Island of Niuafo'ou in the Pacific is one of the remotest places on earth, yet they can call and email anyone in the world.

I was advertising a marketing service to help Pacific Island growers sell their produce in New Zealand in the Tongan Times. I got a shock when I received expressions of interest by email from Niuafo'ou Island!

To give you an idea of how remote the island is, you have to fly from Auckland to Tongatapu Island in Tonga. That is a 2-3 hour flight. Then you either fly to Niuafo'ou Island or take the boat. It is 2-3 hours away from Tongatapu with stopovers in Ha'apai Islands and Vava'u Islands. The boat takes about a week to get there.

The idea of the global theory is the "connectedness" of the whole world by phone, internet, air services and shipping. This idea also proposes that because of this interconnectedness no one should be unemployed.

Like the people of Niuafo'ou, everyone in

the world can have access to overseas markets to sell their goods.

Unfortunately, many internet gurus say that people who market their products on the internet often don't get good results. Probably, despite claims that billions of people are using the internet, most do not buy from internet businesses. They still prefer the corner shop or the local supermarket.

Some internet experts suggest it is due to lack of "expertise" in marketing using the internet. Driving customers to their website or finding the "interested" customers. Even when they attract large numbers of visitors they don't necessarily sell anything because they may not be interested in buying.

When you reach the right people you generate sales, says the experts. Global reach is now possible. Whether for business or to make friends, anyone can do it. Its just a matter of understanding what to do.

CHAPTER 6. STARTING A BUSINESS

In my book **"If you can't find a job start a business"**, some simple ideas are given for starting a business with a small budget if you cannot find a job. There are endless ideas on how to start a small business.

Sometimes you also need a bit of luck.

I decided to start another business. This time without any money. When I started my first business I had saved a small fortune from working for the South Pacific Commission in the Pacific Islands.

I wanted to write. I had always wanted to be a writer since my days at Tonga High School studying Robert Louis Stevenson and the old masters. This time I decided to do it for real.

It is not easy writing and producing books by yourself, but I learned to write and also produce my "homemade" books. I did some research on writing and writers and apparently writers earn the least of all the professionals in New Zealand with an average of $NZ14,000 per year.

I earn a lot less than that. In fact, I made more money in my first year than now, my third year as a writer, but I am hoping to change my luck by doing things better.

I had sent some of my books as samples to many potential agents but they were not interested. Some say that writing and book sales have gone down through the floor because of the internet.

All the bookstores I contacted said they already have their own suppliers.

But I am able to market on the internet in a growing number of websites including amazon.com, blurb.com, apple i-bookstores, wheelersbooks.co.nz and others. So it is a matter of keeping at it and building your reputation and outlets.

When I checked my sales in the

amazon.com kindle bookstore, I had sold 4 ebooks in the last 90 days. That is just one outlet! If I had 100,000 outlets like the bookstores that would be 400,000 books in 90 days!

That is an obvious advantage the bookstores have over the internet. The bookstores get a large number of book lovers coming in everyday and there are a large number of them!.

A writer like J.K.Rowling, author of the famed "Harry Potter series" , for example, is able to sell 300 million copies of her last book because she has access to a large number of bookstores and supermarkets. If there are 1 million shops to sell from around the world....all she has to do is sell 300 books per outlet per year! And she achieves the 300 million! That is just 1 book a day per outlet!

My small writing business is getting bigger and bigger with more and more books and outlets. Hopefully, we can find the secret ingredient to selling millions of books every year! Like J.K.Rowling did. Even if I don't have a million outlets. With the internet, you can sell a million books from one outlet!

So my ideas suggested in **"If you can't find a job start a business"** is working. It's just a matter of keeping at it everyday. "Growing your business" until you achieve the right result.

CHAPTER 7. UNEMPLOYMENT AND WHAT TO DO...

I have suggested the ways and ideas of starting your small business with a small budget. Now obviously, there are other ingredients you need to succeed.

They include;

1. Be persistent
2. Improve your skills
3. Expand your market
4. Try different methods
5. Read and research your topics and areas of need to find the best solutions.
6. Talk to your adviser
7. Don't copy everyone else. Try to do things your way.

Sooner or later, success will come.

I now print my books from USA and the quality is much better. I have overcome the marketability of the books. Now I have to ensure the best possible product and put them out there in the market.

Running your own business also requires a lot of self belief. Many people will put you down and criticize you. Some may be very cruel if they are jealous of you. Just focus on what you have to do and keep doing things better.

If you believe in yourself and what you are doing, you will not lose faith and give up. You will succeed if you believe in your work and others will be convinced by it as well. Even your worst critics will have to acknowledge your work when you become the best at what you do.

I have been told, many times, to get a job! But what those people don't realise is that I started my business because I cannot get the job I want!

I was trained in Science and I became a Scientist in the Pacific Islands for 10 years. I did a lot of good work for the Islands but when I moved to New Zealand, I was unable to replicate my success in the Islands. I attribute this apparent failure at job seeking to my lack of "New Zealand experience". I had left New Zealand after graduation and worked in the Pacific Islands ever since.

The New Zealand job market is very competitive and if employers will have to choose between a Scientist who worked in the Pacific Islands for 10 years and one that worked in New Zealand for 5 years, they will choose the latter; unless you have something special to offer that none of the other applicants have.

I do not feel that I am disadvantaged, even though I earn much less as a writer. I still feel I am in the right career/business, it is just a matter of making it work.

It will be slow as you reinvest every cent you can spare, but overtime you will feel satisfied with the result. The rewards will not all be financial. Most of it will be "kudos" or fame or accolades from the recognition of your work. I prefer to feel satisfied with what I have done, at the end of my career. Rather than making a lot of money and then feeling dissatisfied with it all at the end of it. Feeling that you have wasted your time.

In my case, I do some volunteer work for a charity we established, when I need a break from writing. I think this is important. All writers should have some other distraction to keep them busy when they are not writing books. It is a very intensive exercise so a break is a good idea.

If you do not want to start a business, you can try joining a sports club or church. Very often local jobs are not advertised. Employers prefer to get their new employees from the relatives and friends of their current employees which usually works well for them. You can get employed through the local sport and church network.

Or just canvas the whole town! Go see all potential employers and give them your CV!

CHAPTER 8. YOUR PLAN FOR THE FUTURE

I am a huge advocate of planning your future when you are young. Even if it's just a rough plan.

When I first came from Tonga to New Zealand to further my studies at 17 years of age, I already had a plan. My plan was to get a Bachelor of Science and return to work in Tonga and then do my Master of Science and Doctor of Philosophy later. I had already passed my New Zealand School Certificate and University Entrance Exams in 5 subjects in Tonga in 1978 and 1979.

That was the plan, pass NZSC and UE then go to University in New Zealand to get a degree and get a good job with the Tongan Government.

I did get my Bachelor of Science in 1984 and joined the Tongan Government in June 1985. I was offered a job with the Ministry of Agriculture, Fisheries and Forests as an

Agriculture Officer working in Plant Protection Research.

Although my salary was only $TOP 4,000+ in 1985, I was single and the $163 I got every 2 weeks was more than enough for my needs.

I was earning that much in Auckland, in a week, as a Laborer, but it did not worry me.

In fact the lifestyle as a Government Civil Servant in the islands was very good. Frequent invitations to cocktails and feasts and several overseas trips every year for work was an excellent arrangement for a young man of 24 years.

After 6 years with the Tongan Government, my salary had more than doubled to $9,000+ per year. I joined the Alafua Agricultural Campus of the University of the South Pacific (USP), Samoa, in March 1992. I was already promoted to the post of Senior Plant Virologist with MAFF, Tonga. The "Fellow" position at USP paid $S90,000 per year so it was a huge jump in income. That was $S7500 per month, about $US3,500 or $TOP5,000.

When I joined the South Pacific Commission, I was also appointed as an expert representative at the United Nation's Food and Agriculture Organisation which was the culmination of my short career as a Scientist.

In my job at the South Pacific Commission in 1993, I was making about $NZ1,500 per week or $NZ78,000 per year, about $US66,000.

So I guess I can say my plan worked well.

I think most professionals do plan their future like I did.

Even if you did not do well at school, you can still make a plan.

Many Chief Executives in large companies often started off as Laborers in the company and then work their way up through the years. So you can still succeed even though you only had less than desirable results in High School.

Some of my school mates who did not pass their UE exams with 5 subjects at Tonga High School are now doing very well. One even became a Minister of Education in the Tongan Government! He persisted with his studies and got a PhD!

It is not the end of the world if your plans don't work out at first or you did not do well at school.

Being persistent and trying to do better every time will pay off in the end.

CHAPTER 9. GIVE EVERYONE A MILLION DOLLARS...

Let's expand our idea about "labor assets" and solving the world's problems of poverty and health.

Let's use New Zealand as our model.

If the Government gives all the 4 million residents of New Zealand a million dollars each that will be 4,000 billion dollars or 4 trillion! About the size of the United States of America deficit! But those 4 million residents have an age spread from a year to 90 years or so.

So it won't be so bad if you award the million dollars at 16 years of age, that is only a few thousand kids and it will not break the bank. If you award them as credit rather than cash. That credit is invested and used only in emergencies. The kid can still find a job and the rest of it but when he becomes unemployed the credit is used to employ him or start a business.

Just like the Government giving everyone a $1,000 kick start in Kiwisaver...why not a kickstart of $1 million at 16 years of age!

There isn't much difference in the principle, just the amount.

Boosting the individual's wealth...

I know of at least one country in the world that does that. The tiny Kingdom of Tonga awards a 30 pole town allotment and 8.25 acres of farmland to every male citizen at the age of 16. The Tonga Development Bank can accept loans of up to $TOP30,000 using the farmland as security. So we can say, that the recipient of the properties have boosted his wealth instantly by at least $TOP30,000 thanks to the land awarded to him.

I believe the experts can work it out. This will be the perfect solution to solving the problems of poverty forever.

The Government can manage that money on behalf of the country's citizens and uses the credit for further local development! The huge amount of savings can also help the country develop faster.

All the experts have to do is work out how to increase the amount from the current $1,000 kickstart to $1 million per person into Kiwisaver!

If the AID to the Third World can be "invested" in their youth in this manner, it might be the permanent solutions to poverty they seek. You give them the means to develop themselves.

The reactionary assistance at the moment is just a band aid that will never heal the wound!

CHAPTER 10. ENJOYING LIFE!

After all your plans and business works perfectly, you can put your feet up and relax.

Start enjoying the fruits of your success.

This is how the perfect plan ought to work.

But in reality, most people struggle for most of their lives, tearing their hair out over the smallest problems. Sweating the small stuff as they say.

I would suggest, that even if you achieve just moderate success, you should enjoy every minute of it. Most success that you have will arrive in many forms. So don't expect your success to be just financial rewards.

Most of your success will be overcoming the problems and perfecting your trade. Becoming better and expert at what you do will take many years and mistakes before you will finally get there.

No one can claim they became the best in their fields without mistakes and hours of perfecting their skills. Everyone is fallible and easily mislead unless they take special and extra care in everything they do.

Always be grateful for everything good that comes your way! Sometimes there are good people in your life that you need to acknowledge. Do acknowledge their help.

When you start your business, you will rely heavily on your sponsors. Often, they will be your immediate family. They provide for you while you try and build your business.

Once you succeed, make sure you reward all your sponsors for their help!

Be the best at what you do!

It depends on whether you see the glass as half-full or half-empty.

We are all millionaires!.

OTHER BOOKS FROM RAINBOW ENTERPRISES.

1. Rhymes of an Aspiring Writer+
2. Rhymes of an Aspiring Writer 2
3. The Children of the Gods. The Beginning.
4. The Children of the Gods. The Invasion.
5. The Children of the Gods. The Hurricane's Brothers
6. The art of feeling great*
7. The Rugby Game (Comedy. EBook)*
8. The $999 million heist (Comedy.EBook)*
9. Poetry in Motion. A selection*
10. Where Broken Dreams Fly. A Novel+
11. Po Malu. A Novel*
12. God is Energy. Do you Believe?+
13. God, Genes, Evolution*
14. The Romance*
15. The Children of the Gods. The Beginning and Invasion+

* - these books can be viewed at Blurb.com. Search the author or title in the public bookstore.

+ - available from amazon.com

BOOKS ON HUMOR....

1. Jokes from around the Pacific+
2. Jokes from around the Pacific 2
3. Jokes from around New Zealand
4. Jokes from around Australia
5. The book of rugby jokes+
6. The problem drinkers jokebook
7. The quit smoking jokebook
8. The war on drugs jokebook+
9. Jokes from around the USA
10. Jokes from the Land of the Tikongs
11. Jokes from around New Zealand 2
12. The Stupid Idiot's Jokebook
13. Jokes from around the Pacific. A collection

+ - available from amazon.com

Notes on the author...

Semisi Pone graduated from the University of Auckland in 1985 with a BSc and in 1989 with a MSc (Hons). He has worked as a Scientist in the Pacific for about 10 years and has travelled extensively during that time. He did some work for MAFF, Tonga. University of the South Pacific. South Pacific Commission and the Food and Agriculture Organisation of the United Nations.

He worked in New Zealand during the past 17 years and he has recorded some of his past experience here. He hopes it will motivate or help other people especially those who struggle to find work.

He has written more than 50 books and ebooks. They can be found by searching his name in the websites of amazon.com, blurb.com, apple i-bookstores and wheelersbooks.co.nz. There are others who also sell his books in New Zealand.

He has retired from Science and is a full-time writer. He also does some charity work as the Secretary/Treasurer for the Project Revival Charity Trust (Inc). A charity that produces free online books for disadvantaged kids and youth in Northcote, Auckland, New Zealand.

These free online books are also available to everyone on the planet with access to the internet. Simply log into blurb.com and search Semisi Pone on the website then click on preview on the books you like to read on the list displayed. You can read them for free or buy them.

The Trust hopes to produce up to 50 books for this programme known as the "Dreamtime Stories".

Ebooks are not available for reading. Only 30% of the book is displayed.

www.ingramcontent.com/pod-product-compliance
Lightning Source LLC
Chambersburg PA
CBHW050540210326
41520CB00012B/2653